Piano · Vocal · Guitar

Exclusive Distributors
Folio © 2001 International Music Publications Ltd
Griffin House 161 Hammersmith Road London W6 8BS England

Published 2001
Editor Anna Joyce

Photography Andrew Southam, Len Irish
Other photographs courtesy of Dido

Music arranged by Artemis Music Ltd, Bucks SL0 0NH

MY LOVER'S GONE

my lover's gone, his boots no longer by my door, he left at dawn, and as i slept i felt him go,
returns no more, i will not watch the ocean, my lover's gone, no earthly ships will ever
bring him home again, bring him home again
my lover's gone, i know that kiss will be my last, no more his song, the tune upon his lips has passed
i sing alone, while i watch the ocean, my lover's gone, no earthly ships will ever
bring him home again, bring him home again

HERE WITH ME

i didn't hear you leave, i wonder how am i still here / i don't want to move a thing, it might
change my memory / oh i am what i am, i'll do what i want, but i can't hide / i won't go, i won't
sleep, i can't breathe, until you're resting here with me / i won't leave, i can't hide, i cannot
be, until you're resting here with me / i don't want to call my friends, they might wake me
from this dream / and i can't leave this bed, risk forgetting all that's been / oh i am what i am,
i'll do what i want, but i can't hide / i won't go, i won't sleep, i can't breathe, until you're
resting here with me / i won't leave, i can't hide, i cannot be, until you're resting here with me

ALL YOU WANT

i'd like to watch you sleep at night, to hear you breathe by
my side / and although sleep leaves me behind, there's
nowhere i'd rather be / and now our bed is oh so cold, my
hands feel empty, no one to hold / i can sleep what side i
want, it's not the same with you gone / oh if you'd come
home, i'll let you know that / all you want, is right here in
this room, all you want / and all you need, is sitting here with
you, all you want / it's been three years, one night apart, but
in that night you tore my heart / if only you had slept alone, if
those needs had not been sown / oh you could come home
and you would know that / all you want, is right here in this
room, all you want / all you need is sitting here with you, all
you want / i hear your key turning in the door, i won't be
hearing that sound anymore / and you and your sin can
leave the way you just came in, send my regards to her / i
hope you've found that / all you want, is right there in that
room, all you want / all you need is sitting there with you, all
you want / i'd like to watch you sleep at night, to hear you
breathe by my side

THANKYOU

my tea's gone cold, i'm wondering why i got out of bed at all
the morning rain clouds up my window and i can't see at all
and even if i could it'd be all be grey, but your picture on my wall
it reminds me that it's not so bad, it's not so bad
i drank too much last night, got bills to pay, my head just feels in pain
i missed the bus and there'll be hell today, i'm late for work again
and even if i'm there, they'll all imply that i might not last the day
and then you call me and it's not so bad, it's not so bad and
i want to thank you for giving me the best day of my life
oh just to be with you is having the best day of my life
push the door, i'm home at last and i'm soaking through and through
then you handed me a towel and all i see is you
and even if my house falls down now, i wouldn't have a clue
because you're near me and
i want to thank you for giving me the best day of my life
oh just to be with you is having the best day of my life

HONESTLY OK

i just want to feel safe in my own skin, i just want to be happy again
i just want to feel deep in my own world
but i'm so lonely i don't even want to be with myself anymore
on a different day, if i was safe in my own skin, then i wouldn't feel lost and so frightened
but this is today and i'm lost in my own skin
and i'm so lonely i don't even want to be with myself anymore
i just want to feel safe in my own skin, i just want to be happy again

HUNTER

with one light on in one room, i know you're up when i get home
with one small step upon the stair, i know your look when i get there
if you were a king up there on your throne, would you be wise enough to let me go
for this queen you think you own
wants to be a hunter again, wants to see the world alone again
to take a chance on life again, so let me go
the unread book and painful look, the tv's on, the sound is down
one long pause, then you begin, oh look what the cat's brought in
if you were a king up there on your throne, would you be wise enough to let me go
for this queen you think you own
wants to be a hunter again, wants to see the world alone again
to take a chance on life again, so let me go, let me leave
for the crown you've placed upon my head feels too heavy now
and i don't know what to say to you but i'll smile anyhow
and all the time i'm thinking, thinking
i want to be a hunter again, want to see the world alone again
to take a chance on life again, so let me go

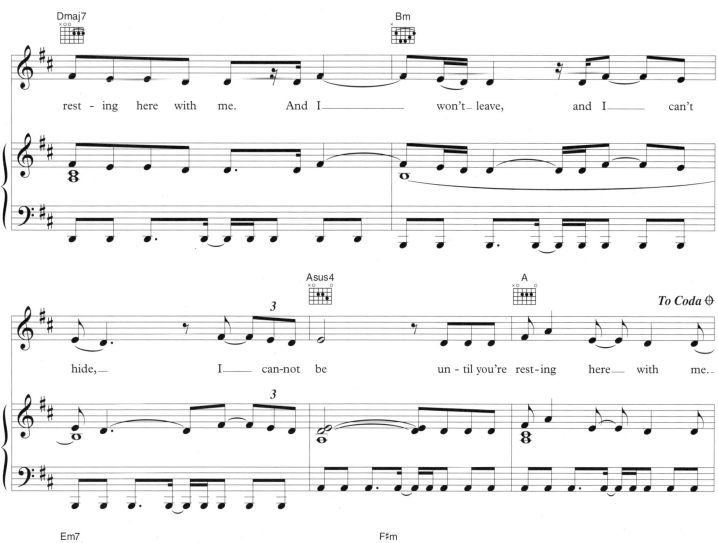

rest - ing here with me. And I_____ won't_ leave, and I_____ can't

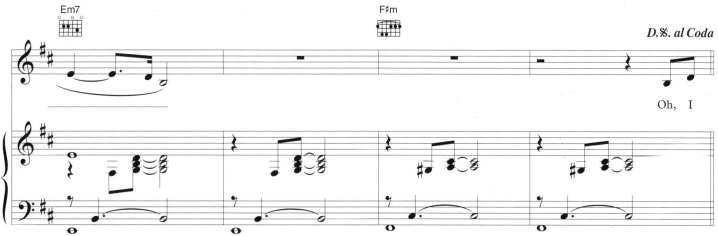

hide,___ I____ can-not be un - til you're rest - ing here__ with me.__

To Coda ⊕

D.%. al Coda

Oh, I

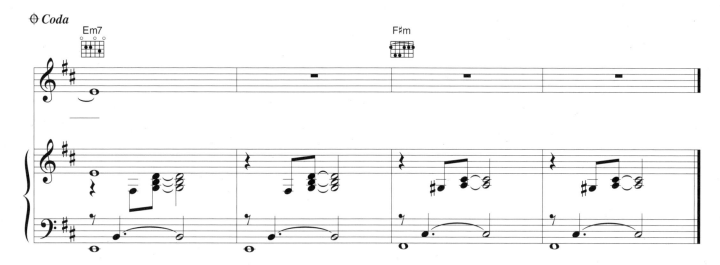

⊕ *Coda*

DON'T THINK OF ME

Words and Music by
Dido Armstrong, Rollo Armstrong,
Pauline Taylor and Paul Herman

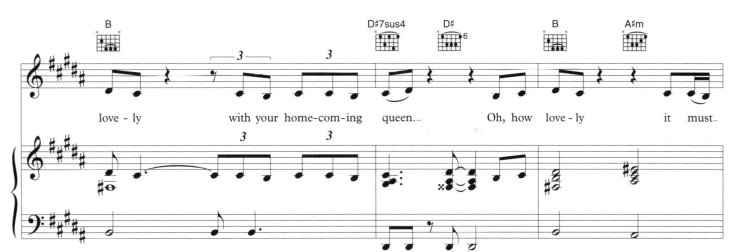

don't think of— me.—— And when she lays———— in your

warm arms———— don't think of— me.————

2. So you're with her—— and not with me— I know she

spreads— sweet— ho— ney.—— In fact your best friend, I—— heard he

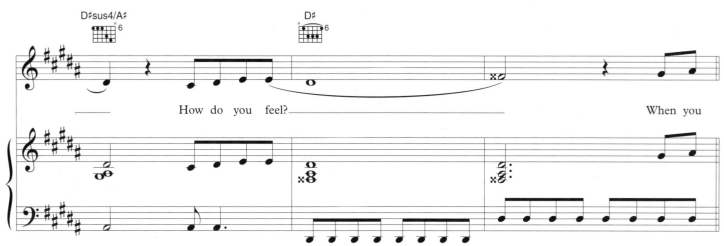

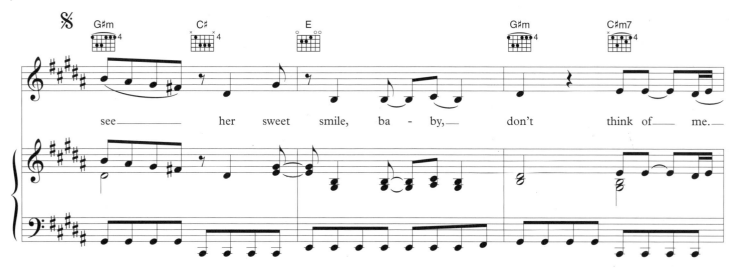

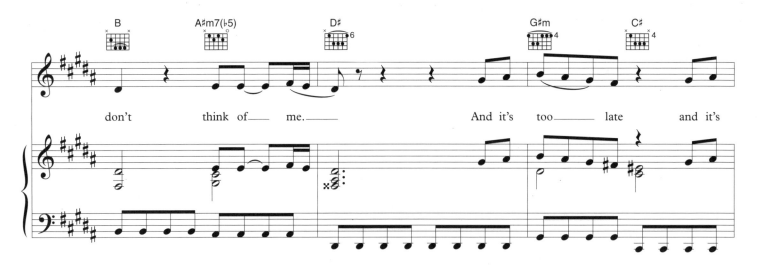

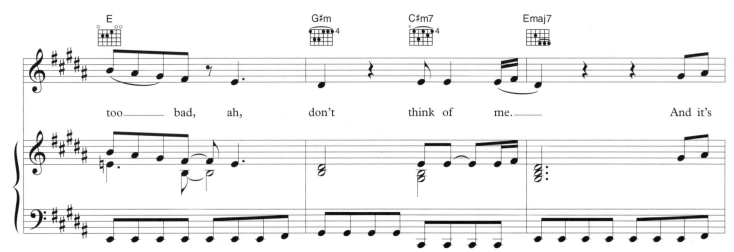

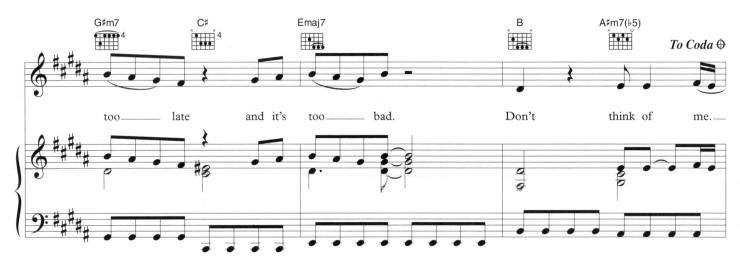

HUNTER

Words and Music by
Dido Armstrong and
Rollo Armstrong

king up there on your throne, would you be wise e-nough to let me

go. For this queen you think you own wants to wants to

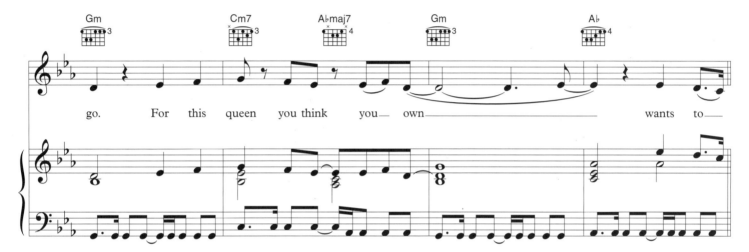

be a hun - ter a-gain. I want to see the world a - lone a - gain,

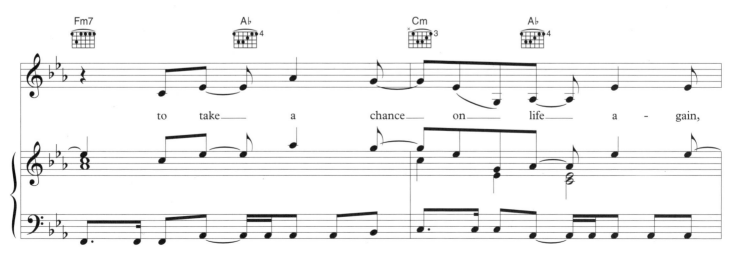

to take a chance on life a - gain,

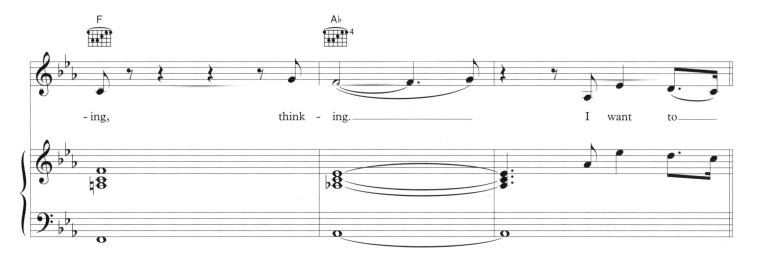

-ing, think - ing. I want to

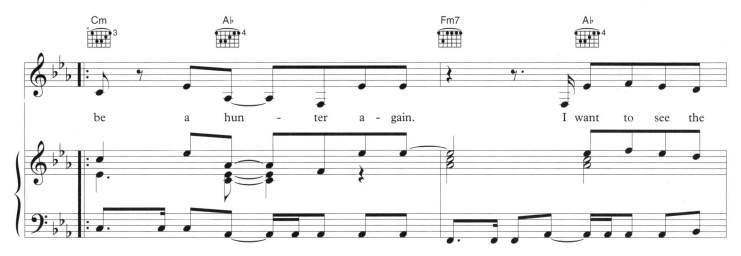

be a hun - ter a - gain. I want to see the

world a - lone a - gain, to take a chance on life a - gain,

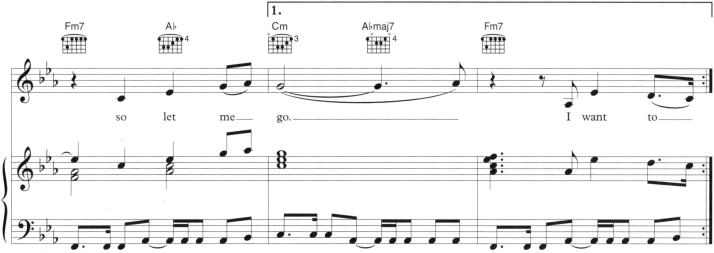

1.

so let me go. I want to

go._____ Let me___ leave._____

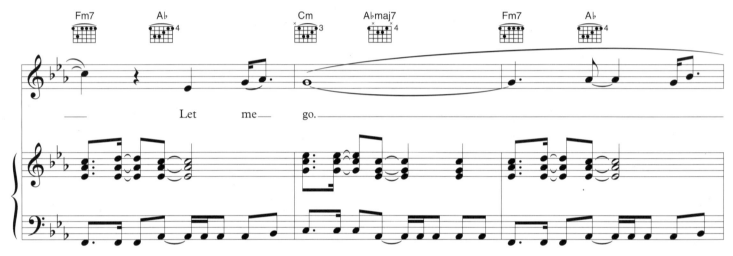

___ Cm Let me___ go._____

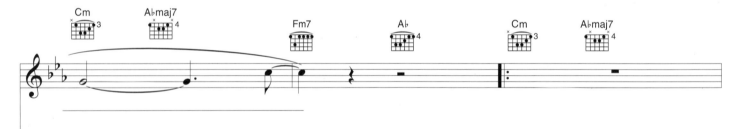

Repeat ad lib. to fade

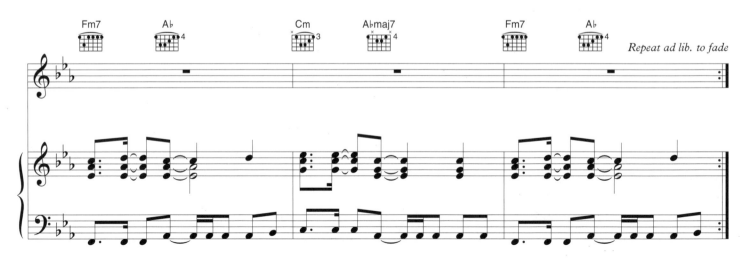

THANKYOU

Words and Music by
Dido Armstrong and
Paul Herman

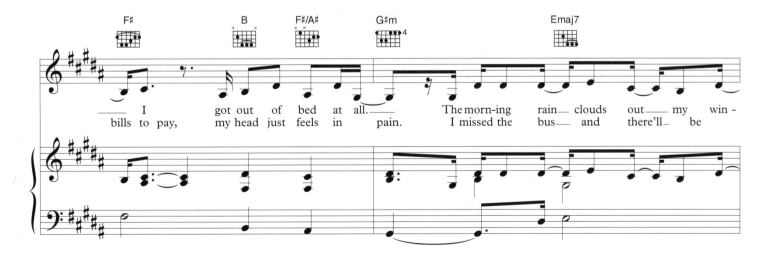

22

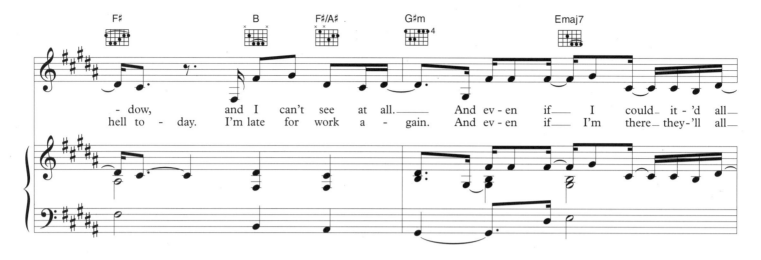

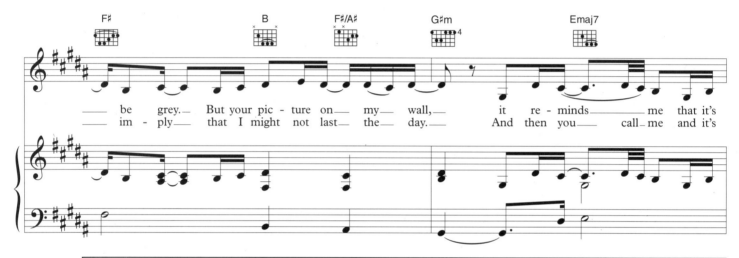

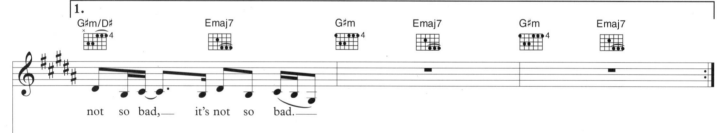

MY LOVER'S GONE

Words and Music by
Dido Armstrong and
Jamie Catto

1. My lov-er's gone, his boots no long-er by my door.

He left at dawn, and as I slept I felt him go.

Re-turns no more, I will not watch the o-cean.

My lov-er's gone,— no earth-ly— ships— will ev-er bring

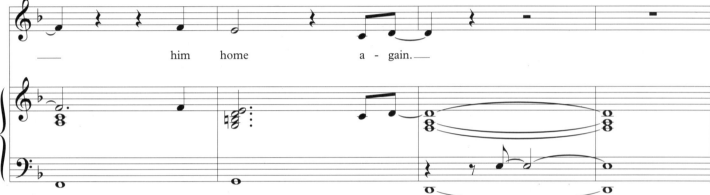

— him home a - gain.—

Bring him— home a - gain.—

2. My lov-er's gone,— I know that kiss— will be— my last.
3. My lov-er's gone,— his boots— no long-er by— my door.

28

No more his song,⏤ the tune⏤ up - on⏤ his⏤ lips⏤ has passed.
He left⏤ at dawn,⏤ and as⏤ I slept⏤ I felt⏤ him go.⏤

⏤ I sing a - lone,⏤ while I watch⏤ the o - cean.
Re - turns⏤ no more,⏤ I will not watch the o - cean.

My lov - er's gone.⏤ no earth - ly⏤ ships⏤ will ev - er bring

⏤ him home a - gain.⏤

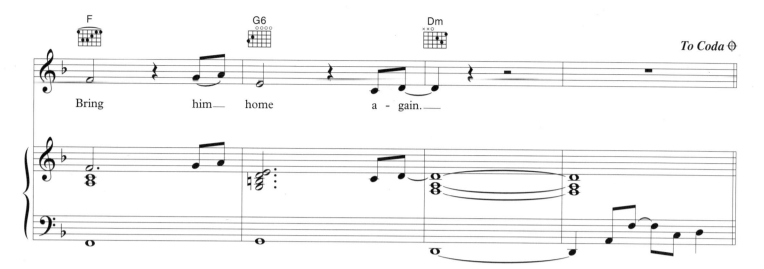

Bring him home a - gain.

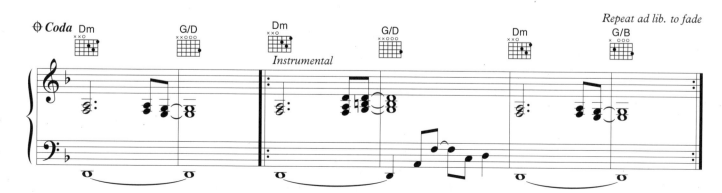

ALL YOU WANT

**Words and Music by
Dido Armstrong, Paul Herman
and Rollo Armstrong**

2. And now our bed is oh,— so cold, my hands feel emp-ty. No one to hold.—
3. It's been three years, one night a-part,— but in that night— you tore my heart.

And I can sleep what side— I want, it's not the same— with you gone.—
If on - ly you had slept a - lone, if those seeds had not been

sown.
Oh,— if you'd come home— I'll let— you know— that
Oh,— you could come home— and you— would know— that

all— you— want is right here in this— room. All— you—
(% there in that—)

HONESTLY OK

Words and Music by
Dido Armstrong,
Matthew Benbrook and
Rollo Armstrong

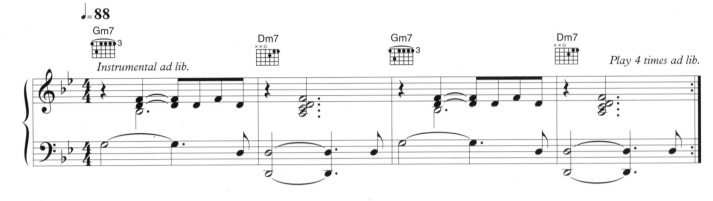

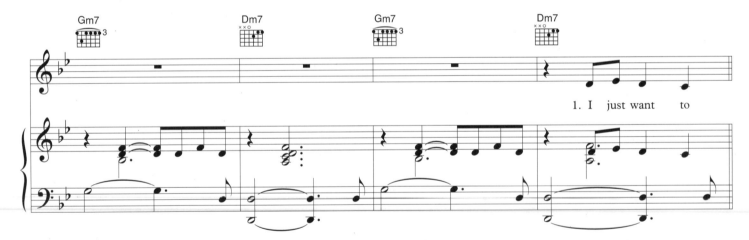

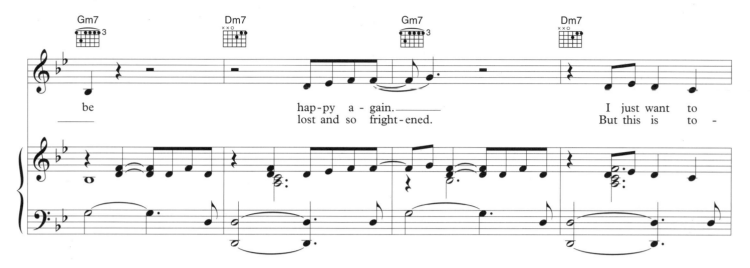

be _____   hap-py a - gain. _____   I just want to
         lost and so fright-ened.   But this is to -

feel   deep in my own ___ world.   But I'm so
- day   and I'm lost in my own ___ skin.   And I'm so

Accordion

lone - ly I don't ev - en wan-na be with my-self a - ny - more. ___

1.

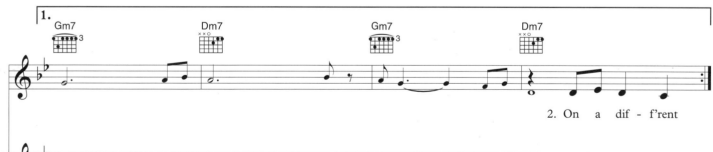

2. On a dif - f'rent

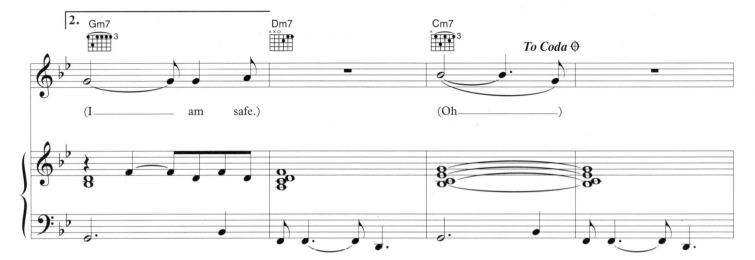

(I____ am safe.) (Oh____)

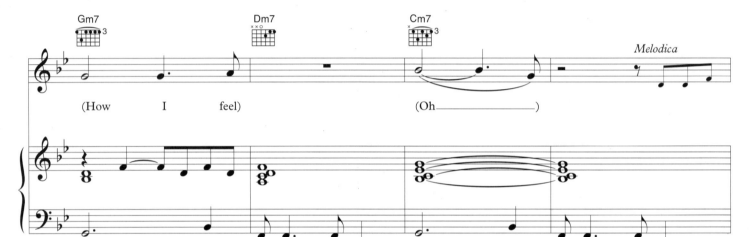

(How I feel) (Oh____)

And I'm so

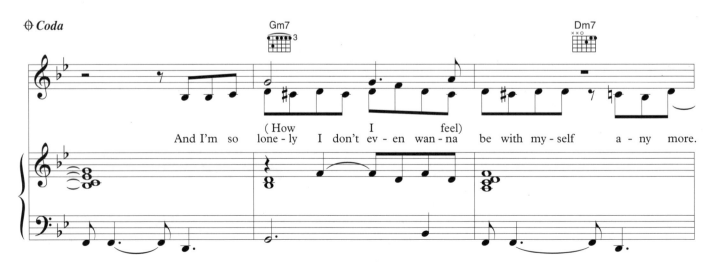

And I'm so lone-ly I don't ev-en wan-na be with my-self a-ny more.
(How I feel)

SLIDE

Words and Music by
Dido Armstrong and
Paul Herman

ISOBEL

Words and Music by
Dido Armstrong and
Rollo Armstrong

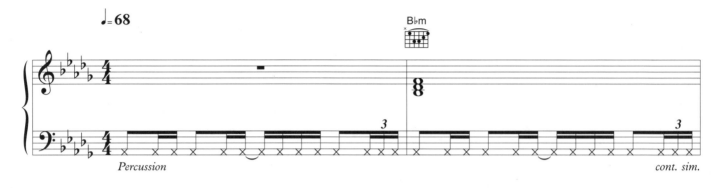

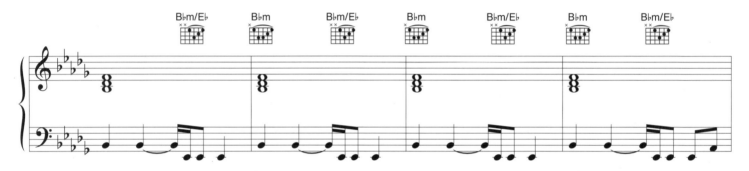

1. I thought it was fun-ny when you missed the train.
2. And who he would be-come, all the things he'd have done,

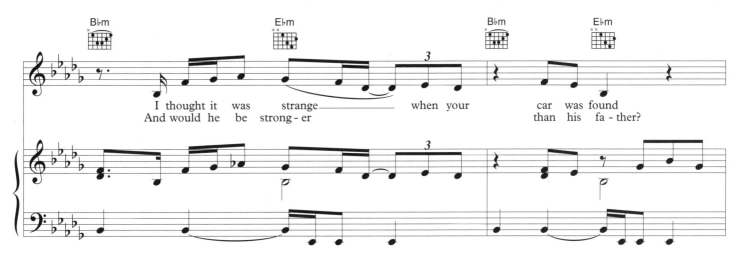

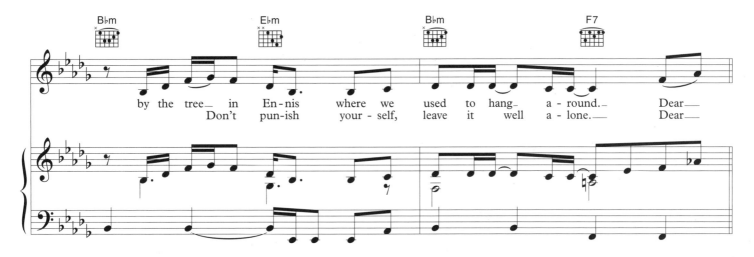

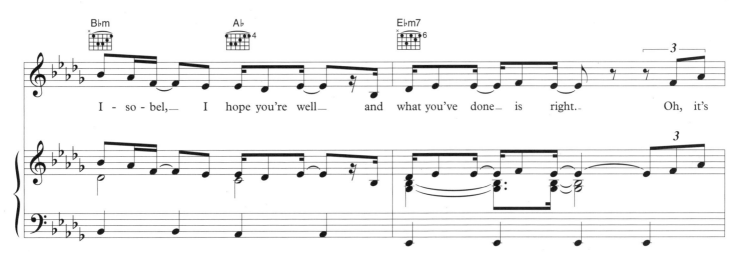

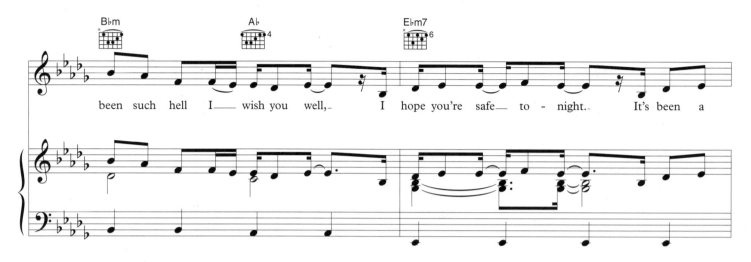

been such hell I — wish you well, — I hope you're safe — to - night. — It's been a

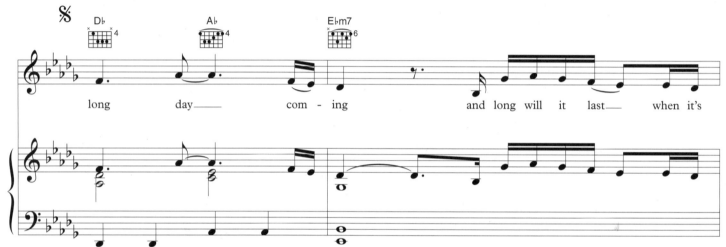

long day — com - ing and long will it last — when it's

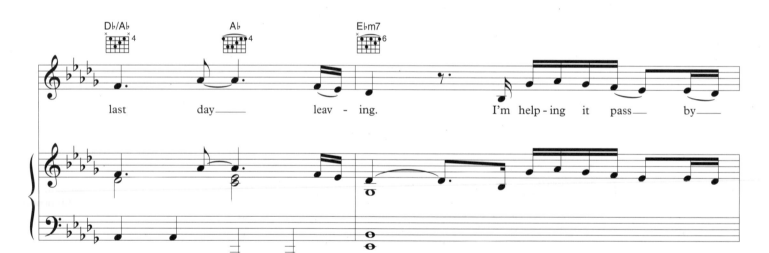

last day — leav - ing. I'm help-ing it pass — by —

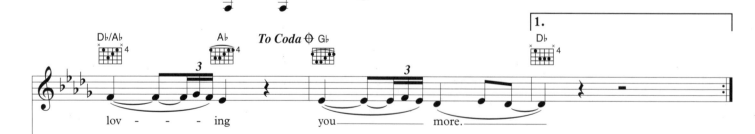

To Coda ⊕ G♭

1.

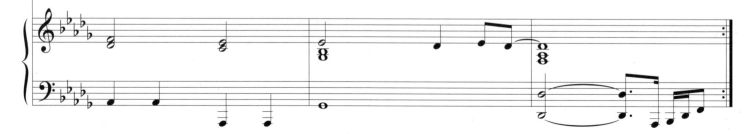

lov - - ing you — more. —

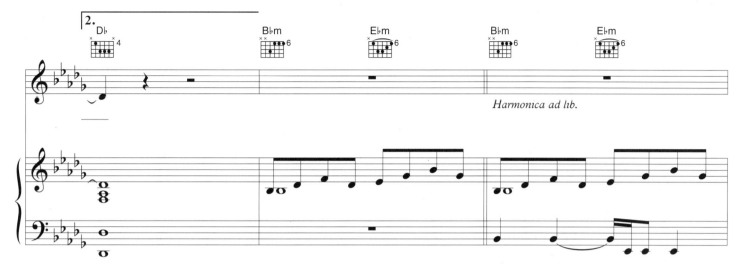

Harmonica ad lib.

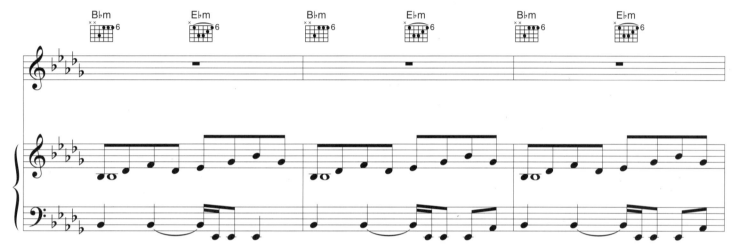

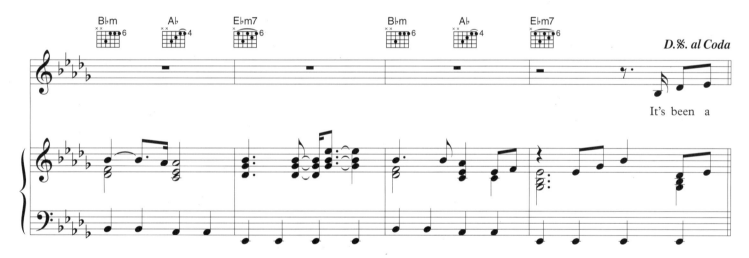

D.%. al Coda

It's been a

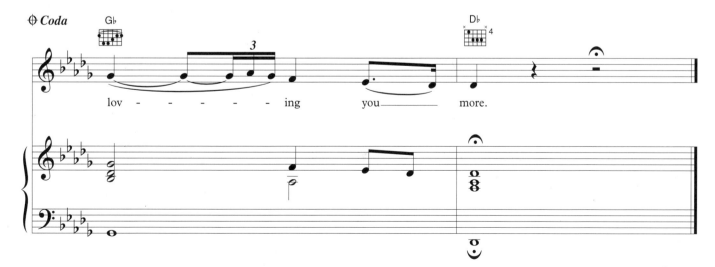

lov - - - - ing you⸺⸺ more.

I'M NO ANGEL

**Words and Music by
Dido Armstrong, Paul Statham
and Pascal Gabriel**

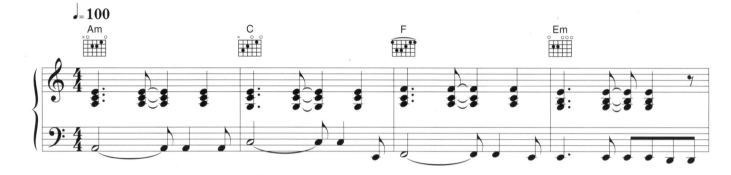

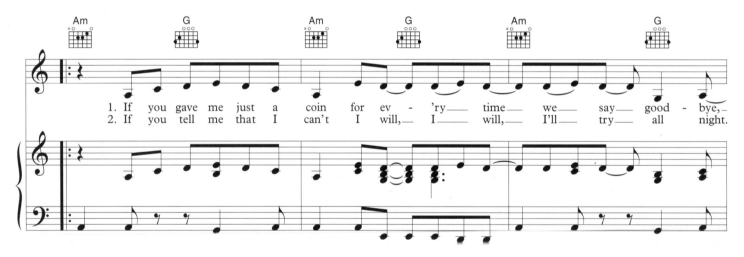

1. If you gave me just a coin for ev - 'ry____ time____ we____ say____ good - bye,
2. If you tell me that I can't I will,____ I____ will, I'll____ try____ all____ night.

well I'd be rich be - yond my dreams. I'm sor - ry____ for
And if I say I'm com - ing home I'll prob - ab - ly____

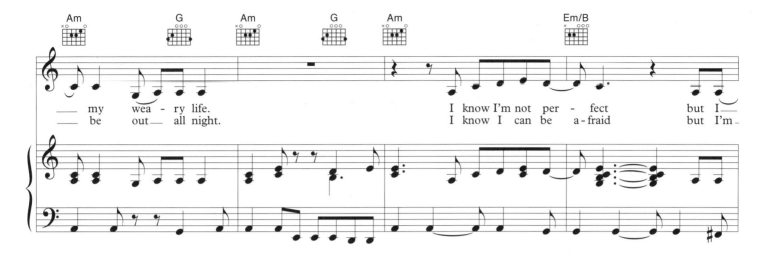

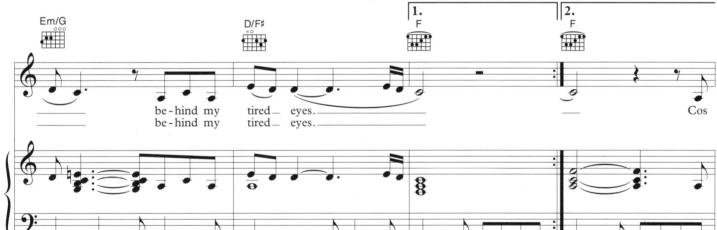

I'm _____ no an - gel, but does that mean that I can live _____ my life. _____

I'm _____ no an - gel, but please don't think that I can't cry. _____ Ah. _____

To Coda ⊕

I'm _____ no an - gel, but does that mean that I won't fly? _____

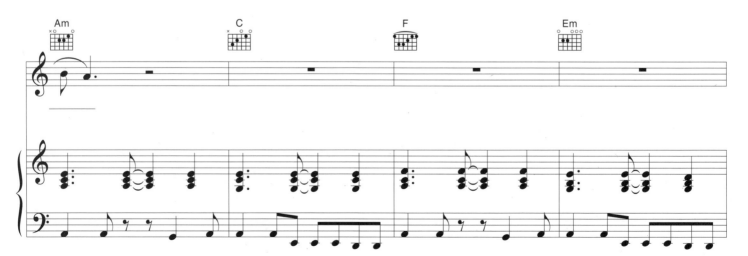

TAKE MY HAND

Words and Music by
Dido Armstrong and
Richard Dekkard

top of the world__ and tell me how__ you're feel - ing. What you feel__ is

what I feel__ for__ you.__ Take my hand_____ and if I'm ly-ing_____ to you,__ I'll

al-ways be a - lone,__ if I'm ly-ing to you._____

1, 2.

Repeat ad lib.

N.C.

Guitar ad lib.

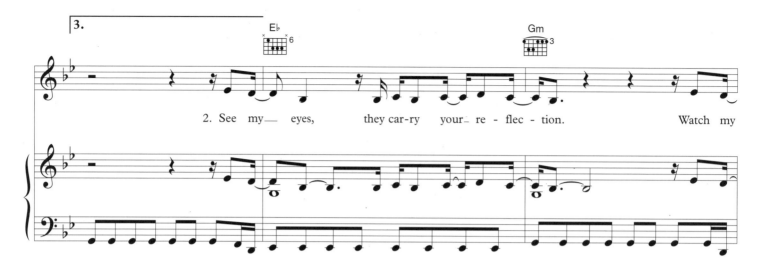

2. See my eyes, they car-ry your re - flec - tion. Watch my

lips and hear the words I'm tell-ing you. Give your

trust to me and look in - to my heart. And

show me, and show me what you're do - ing. So sit on

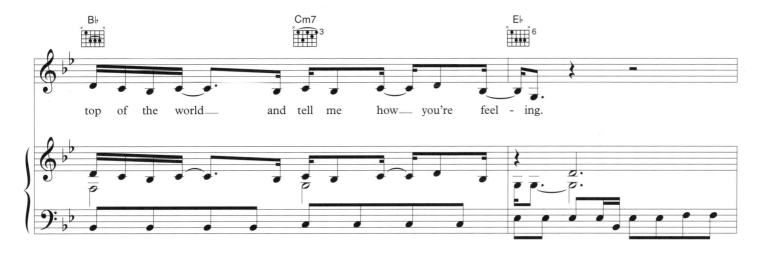

top of the world___ and tell me how___ you're feel - ing.

What you feel_ is what I feel_ for_ you.___ Take my hand___ and if I'm

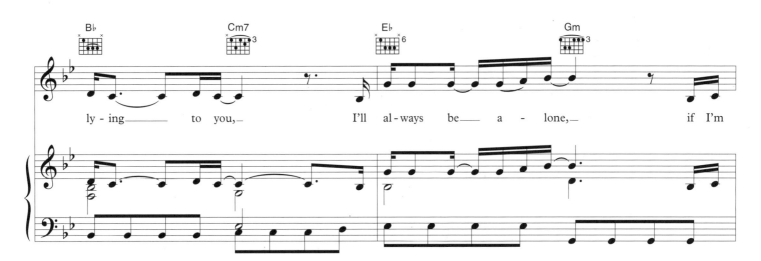

ly - ing___ to you,_ I'll al - ways be a - lone,___ if I'm

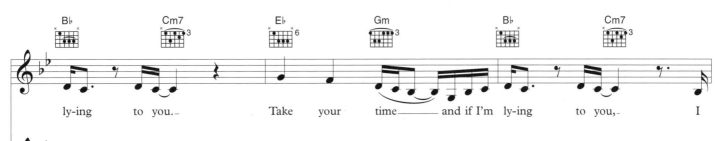

ly-ing to you._ Take your time___ and if I'm ly-ing to you,_ I

know you'll_ find that you be-lieve_ me, you be-lieve_ me, you be-lieve_ me.__

You be-lieve_ me._____

Violins 8ᵛᵃ

1° Tacet

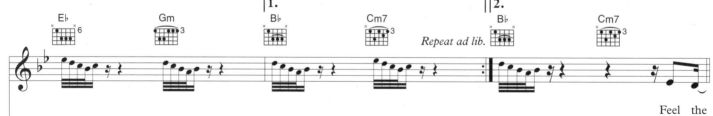

1. **2.**

Repeat ad lib.

Feel the

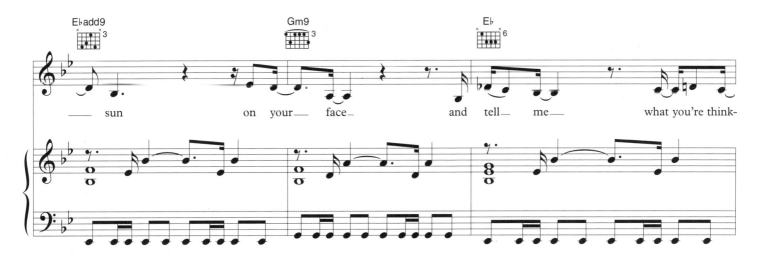

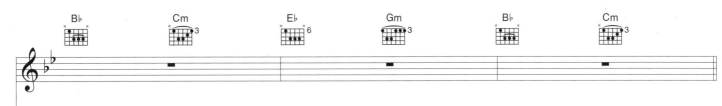

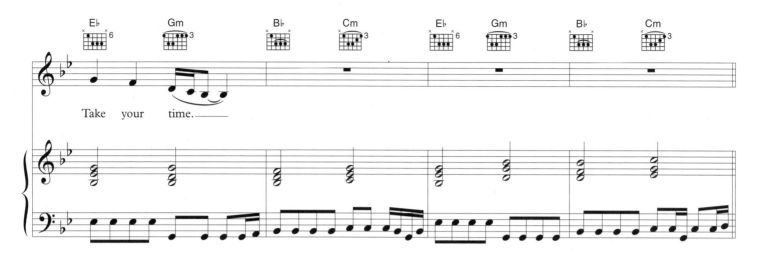

Take your time.——

Take my hand——— and if I'm ly-ing——— to you,— I'll

al-ways be— a - lone,— if I'm ly-ing to you.— Take your time——— and if I'm

1.

ly-ing to you,— I know you'll— find that you be-lieve—me.

you be-lieve me. You be-lieve me. You be-lieve me._ You be lieve_ me._

You be-lieve_ me._ You be-lieve_ me._

MY LIFE

Words and Music by
Dido Armstrong, Mark Bates and
Rollo Armstrong

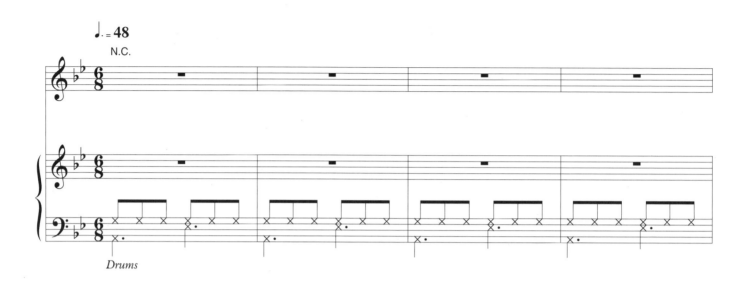

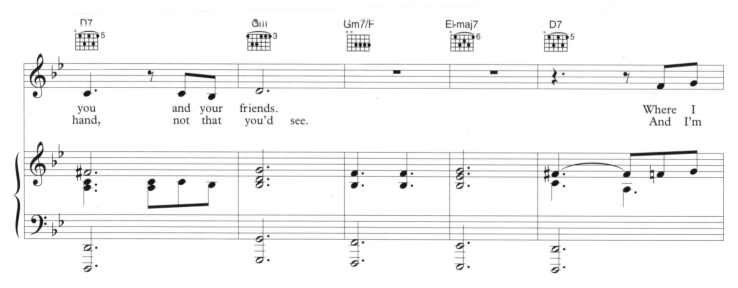

life.

It's my life.

(It's my life.)

Piano solo ad lib.